EARTH'S TREASURES

JADE

CHRISTINE PETERSEN

ABDO Publishing Company

visit us at
www.abdopublishing.com

Published by ABDO Publishing Company, PO Box 398166, Minneapolis, MN 55439.
Copyright © 2014 by Abdo Consulting Group, Inc. International copyrights reserved in all
countries. No part of this book may be reproduced in any form without written permission from the
publisher. The Checkerboard Library™ is a trademark and logo of ABDO Publishing Company.

Printed in the United States of America, North Mankato, Minnesota.
052013
092013

 PRINTED ON RECYCLED PAPER

Cover Photo: iStockphoto
Interior Photos: Alamy pp. 5, 9, 29; AP Images pp. 4, 21; Getty Images p. 29;
    Glow Images pp. 13, 25; iStockphoto pp. 1, 18–19, 25; Science Source pp. 15, 17, 20, 22–23,
    23, 27; SuperStock pp. 6–7, 11, 17; Thinkstock p. 8

Editors: Rochelle Baltzer, Megan M. Gunderson
Art Direction: Neil Klinepier

Library of Congress Control Number: 2013932663

Cataloging-in-Publication Data

Petersen, Christine.
 Jade / Christine Petersen.
  p. cm. -- (Earth's treasures)
ISBN 978-1-61783-872-9
Includes bibliographical references and index.
1. Jade--Juvenile literature.   2. Gems--Juvenile literature.   3. Mineralogy--Juvenile literature.   I.
Title.
553.8--dc23
                                                                    2013932663

CONTENTS

SYMBOL OF POWER

Can you imagine becoming a king or queen at the age of 12? That is what happened to Pakal. Pakal was born in 603 CE. His kingdom was Palenque in what is now Mexico. It was part of the ancient Maya civilization.

A Maya king wore jade as a symbol of power. Only the most important Maya could wear jade. The king wore a beautiful jade belt and headband. His teeth had bits of jade fitted in them. He wore jade necklaces, pendants, and collars.

Pakal's funeral mask was made of more than 200 pieces of jade and other stones.

As an older man, Pakal ordered a stone pyramid to be built. This would be his tomb. The people of Palenque expected their king to be reborn as a god, like the Sun is reborn each day. When Pakal died, they dressed his body in jade. There were rings on each finger and ornaments on his ears. Pakal wore jade bracelets and held a jade cube. He had a jade bead in his mouth.

Palenque

In 1949, **archaeologist** Alberto Ruz Lhuillier was studying the ruins of Palenque. Ruz hoped to find objects that would explain the lives of ancient Maya people. He found a secret stairway leading into the heart of Pakal's pyramid. At the base of the stairway was a large room. Nine huge statues guarded a stone coffin. Inside were the bones of King Pakal, still wearing his treasured jade jewelry.

5

WHAT IS JADE?

Ancient people survived by using materials they found in nature. They built wooden houses and burned logs for warmth. Plant fibers and animal furs were used to make clothing. Salt was used to preserve food. Copper could be shaped into tools. Turquoise made beautiful jewelry.

Can you guess what salt, copper, and turquoise have in common with jade? They are all minerals. Several thousand different minerals have been identified on Earth.

Minerals share certain qualities. They are typically solid rather than liquid or gaseous. They are usually inorganic. This means they were made in the earth rather than by living things.

Every mineral contains one or more chemical elements. Microscopic atoms are the building blocks of

elements. They link together in repeating patterns to form three-dimensional crystals. Copper contains only copper atoms. Rock salt is made of the elements sodium and chlorine. Jade is made up of many different elements.

Jade has been used to create treasured objects for thousands of years.

LONG HISTORY

The Maori of New Zealand found tiny pebbles and giant boulders of green jade around their local streams. They named it pounamu.

The Maori made knives, fishhooks, and spear points from this durable mineral. They passed these tools down from generation to generation. Objects made from pounamu were treasured as reminders of their past. The stone was prized for both its strength and its beauty.

In western Canada, native peoples made **celts** from their supply of jade. These tools were shaped like ax heads and used as scrapers. **First Nations** peoples sometimes traded their jade celts like money. They also placed them in graves as gifts for the dead.

Other common names for pounamu are greenstone and New Zealand jade.

Jade has been used in China for at least 5,000 years. Chinese craftsmen shaped the stone into vessels, jewelry, statues, and animal figures. Jade also was important in religious ceremonies.

When Prince Liu Sheng was buried in 113 BCE, he wore a jade suit of armor. It was built from almost 2,500 tiny squares of jade. The pieces were sewn together with gold wire. His people may have believed jade would protect the prince's body from evil spirits and decay.

Jade suits have been unearthed in different parts of China.

9

ANCIENT LAPIDARY

The Olmec of what is now southern Mexico may have been the first people to use jade in North America. They especially prized a supply of blue-green jade. It came from the Motagua Valley in what is now Guatemala.

In 1989, **archaeologists** studied an Olmec site called El Manatí. More than 3,600 years ago, Olmec people built a shrine there. Worshippers placed jade **celts** and beads into a pool as part of a ritual.

Olmec artists faced a problem when working with jade. This mineral was too hard to be cut or carved. Instead, it had to be ground down.

The lapidary was a craftsman specially trained to work with jade and other minerals. First, he used a saw made of stone, wood, or string to cut a piece off of a jade boulder. Then the lapidary used drills to create holes. He used sandstone saws to scratch delicate designs such as facial features onto the surface.

Polishing the hard stone took much time. The lapidary may have used deer hide with gritty quartz sand or powdered jade to do this. After thousands of repeated movements, the object gleamed.

In Chinese, the phrase for jade work is cho mo. *This means "grinding and polishing."*

CONQUERED

Conquistador Hernán Cortés moved from Spain to the island of Hispaniola as a young man. In 1511, he helped conquer Cuba. In 1519, he sailed to Mexico in search of gold. Cortés sailed west from Cuba with more than 500 soldiers. His ships landed at Tabasco, along the Gulf of Mexico.

At that time, the Aztec people ruled much of what is now Mexico. Aztec emperor Montezuma II did not want these invaders in his kingdom. He quickly sent a trusted adviser to Cortés. The man presented Cortés with precious stones, feather objects, and jade beads.

"These rich stones . . . should be sent to your Emperor," the Aztec man told Cortés. "They are of the greatest value, each one being esteemed more highly than a great load of gold."

But Cortés did not want jade. Montezuma was relieved Cortés only wanted gold, because Montezuma valued jade much more highly. But then, the Spaniards conquered Montezuma's city and took all the gold they found.

12

The Aztecs believed that jade could cure illnesses. In time, this caught the interest of the Spaniards. Supplies of jade were shipped to Europe as a kind of medicine. In time, Europeans also learned to appreciate this stone for its natural beauty.

Cortés meeting Montezuma

TWO JADES

French **mineralogist** Alexis Damour was curious about jade. He had already looked at samples from China. He found this jade to be **dense** and tough. This mineral was a **silicate** of calcium and magnesium. It was made of fine fibers or needlelike crystals that wound around each other like tangled hair. This explained why the mineral was so tough.

In 1863, Damour was given a piece of jade from Myanmar. It looked and felt much like the Chinese jade. But his microscope told a different story. This new sample was a silicate of sodium and aluminum. Its crystals were granular. Clearly the two jades were not the same mineral. Damour called the grainy form jadeite. The kind with stringy crystals was nephrite.

Jadeite is a 6.5 to 7 on the Mohs hardness scale. Nephrite is a 5.5 to 6.

14

MOHS HARDNESS SCALE

MOHS HARDNESS	MINERAL	HARDNESS OF OTHER MATERIALS
1	talc	
2	gypsum	2.2 fingernail
3	calcite	3.2 copper penny
4	fluorite	
5	apatite	5.1 pocketknife
6	orthoclase	6.5 steel needle
7	quartz	7.0 streak plate
8	topaz	
9	corundum	
10	diamond	

S O F T E S T → H A R D E S T

Both jadeite and nephrite may be white or colorless.

CHANGING ROCK

Whether jadeite or nephrite, where does jade come from? Earth's rocky outer crust is like a giant jigsaw puzzle. It is made up of several large pieces called plates. The plates float side-by-side atop the hot mantle.

As Earth's giant plates move, they may crash into or slide against each other. Or, one plate may move over another. The lower plate is forced down into the mantle.

Water and minerals are squeezed out of the rock as it moves downward. This mineral-rich fluid seeps upward into the overlying plate. Jadeite is formed there under great pressure. Nephrite is also formed when old rocks become new rock. This takes much pressure and high temperatures. This means both types of jade are metamorphic rock.

Over time, rain, ice, and wind cause rock to crack and crumble. This process of erosion causes jade boulders to tumble downhill. They become mixed with common stones in streambeds. Much jade has been found out in the open like this.

The most valuable jadeite is still found in Myanmar. In fact, this is the world's most valuable gem. It costs even more than diamonds! Small deposits of jadeite can also be found in China, Japan, Guatemala, and California.

Nephrite is found in several areas, including China, New Zealand, and parts of Europe. It can also be found in western North America, including British Columbia, Alaska, California, and Wyoming.

Nephrite

Jadeite

North America

South America

Top Jade-Producing Countries

- Austria
- Canada
- China
- Japan
- Myanmar
- New Zealand
- United States

Europe

Asia

Africa

Australia

N
W E
S

A REAL GEM

Both nephrite and jadeite are used as gemstones. Gems are minerals used for jewelry or decoration. They are special because they are durable, rare, and beautiful.

Jadeite and nephrite are both exceptionally durable minerals. Jadeite is harder than nephrite. However, nephrite is the toughest mineral. This means it is not brittle and will not easily shatter. That is why it was so useful for ax heads and other tools.

The crystal structures of the two kinds of jade make them look different. This makes it easier for people to tell the two apart if polished. Both have a beautiful **luster**, but jadeite appears glassy. Nephrite looks oily instead.

A beautifully carved jade figurine

20

This jade bracelet is worth more than $1 million.

MORE THAN GREEN

Color lends beauty to gemstones. Pure jade of either variety is frosty white. But most people think green when they think of jade!

A change in color is caused by impurities. Tiny amounts of other elements enter the crystal structure during its formation. Large amounts of iron can turn nephrite black. A little bit of iron causes jadeite to become pale green. Emerald green jadeite occurs when chromium replaces aluminum in some of the crystals.

Jadeite comes in more colors than nephrite. In fact, there is even rainbow jadeite! This jade has multiple colors in the same stone. Still, the most prized color of jade is emerald green.

Honey jadeite

Polished green jadeite

MAORI JADE

Lapidaries are the lucky people who get to work with gem-quality jade. The Maori people of New Zealand are considered the finest lapidaries of nephrite jade. This pounamu is still an important part of their **culture**.

A Maori gem worker has access to all of the technology of the modern world. Helicopters are used to move heavy pounamu boulders. A large diamond saw can slice the stone far faster than in ancient times!

Next, the piece of jade is held against a fast-spinning, **abrasive** wheel. The wheel's edge is coated in dust made from something harder than jade. That hard grit **scours** the jade, shaping its surface bit by bit. Finally, the lapidary uses a diamond-tipped instrument to scratch fine details into the stone.

Back in 1840, the British colonized New Zealand. The government soon took control of valuable pounamu deposits. Maori people fought for more than 100 years against this unfair treatment.

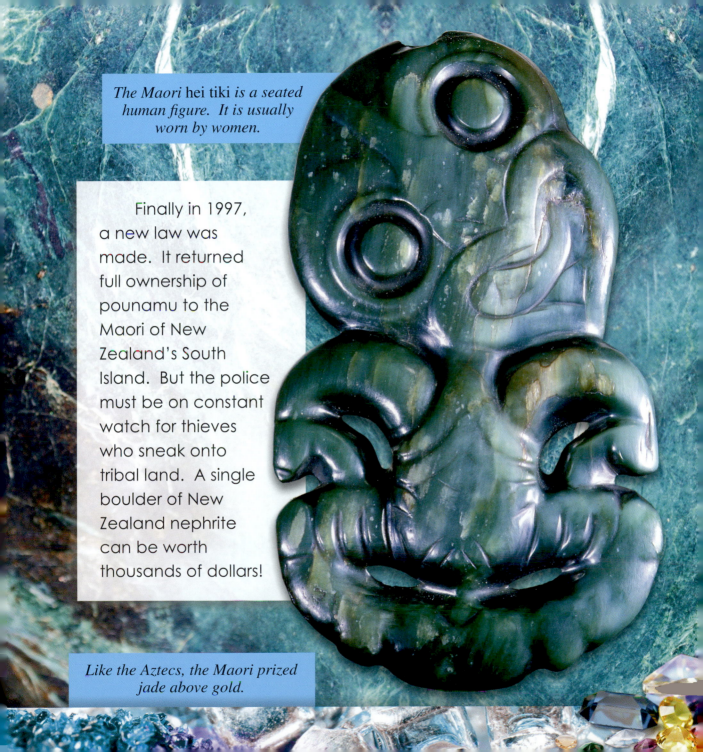

The Maori hei tiki *is a seated human figure. It is usually worn by women.*

Finally in 1997, a new law was made. It returned full ownership of pounamu to the Maori of New Zealand's South Island. But the police must be on constant watch for thieves who sneak onto tribal land. A single boulder of New Zealand nephrite can be worth thousands of dollars!

Like the Aztecs, the Maori prized jade above gold.

IMITATION OR NOT?

Visit a jewelry store and you'll find **synthetic** diamonds and rubies for sale alongside natural stones. Synthetic gems are identical to natural minerals. They have the same chemical structure and may be just as beautiful. The only difference is that synthetic gems are made in a laboratory.

There are many ways to imitate beautiful, expensive jade. These fakes look like jade, but they are made from different chemical elements.

Some types of serpentine are sold as jade. However, this mineral is softer than real jade. Bowenite is often mistaken for nephrite or used in its place. This mineral is formed under similar conditions as jade. It has the same solid, smooth texture and range of colors. It can be used as jewelry under its own name, too.

True jade is sometimes changed to improve its appearance before sale. The stone may be waxed to bring out its shine. Dyes can be added to change the color of a natural stone. Even heavy lead glass can be tinted to look like emerald-green jade!

Bowenite is the state mineral of Rhode Island.

FINDING JADE

If you like jade, why not attend the Big Sur Jade Festival? This event is held each October on the California coastline near Monterey Bay. Lapidaries come from around the world to show their work. Bring some spending money. You may want to take home a piece of carved jade!

While you're there, make a stop at Jade Cove. You must be a good hiker to reach this beach. Plan to go with adults who are also comfortable in the outdoors.

Jade Cove is safest at low tide. Wear hiking boots or sneakers to protect your feet. You will walk a coastal trail and scrabble

Become a Rock Hound!

WOULD YOU LIKE TO START YOUR OWN COLLECTION OF GEMS AND MINERALS? BECOME A ROCK HOUND!

To get started, locate a site likely to have the treasures you seek. Before you head out, be sure it is legal and you have permission to collect specimens from your search area. Then, gather the tools and safety gear you'll need. Don't forget to bring an adult!

Label your treasures with the date and location you found them. Many rock hounds set a goal for their collections. For example, they might gather samples of all the minerals found in their state or province.

Finally, always leave the land in better shape than you found it. Respecting the environment helps preserve it for future rock hounds and the rest of your community.

WHAT WILL YOU NEED?

- map
- compass
- magnifying glass
- hard hat or bicycle helmet
- safety goggles
- sunscreen
- bucket
- shovel
- rock hammer
- pan or screen box
- containers for your finds

down a steep hillside to reach the beach. It is worth the effort! You can wander or wade in search of nephrite pebbles.

In Jade Cove, jade can be collected without a mining permit. But remember to only take what you can carry. If visitors are not too greedy, the supply of nephrite may last for years to come. Perhaps someday you'll return to show your children this treasure of the earth.

Jade Cove is part of the Los Padres National Forest and the Monterey Bay National Marine Sanctuary.

29

GLOSSARY

abrasive - something used to rub or wear away by friction.

archaeologist (ahr-kee-AH-luh-jihst) - one who studies the remains of people and activities from ancient times.

celt - an ancient object shaped like an ax head.

culture - the customs, arts, and tools of a nation or a people at a certain time.

dense - having a high mass per unit volume.

First Nations - Native Americans of Canada.

luster - a shiny quality, especially from reflected light.

mineralogist - a scientist who studies minerals.

scour - to rub hard with a rough material.

silicate - a mineral that contains silicon and oxygen.

synthetic - relating to something that is human-made by a chemical process.

SAYING IT

lapidary - LA-puh-dehr-ee
Maori - MOWR-ee
metamorphic - meh-tuh-MAWR-fihk

WEB SITES

To learn more about jade, visit ABDO Publishing Company online. Web sites about jade are featured on our Book Links page. These links are routinely monitored and updated to provide the most current information available.

www.abdopublishing.com

INDEX